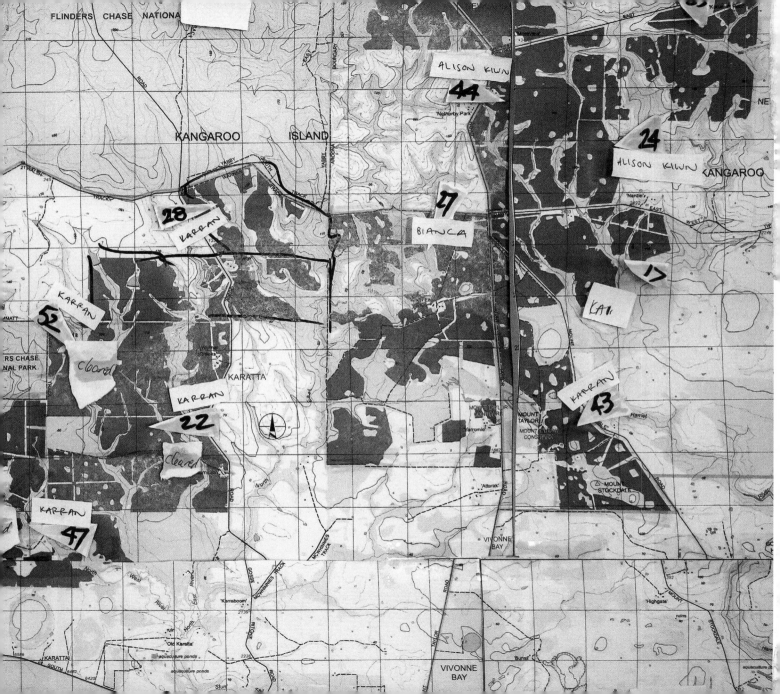

The 99th Koala

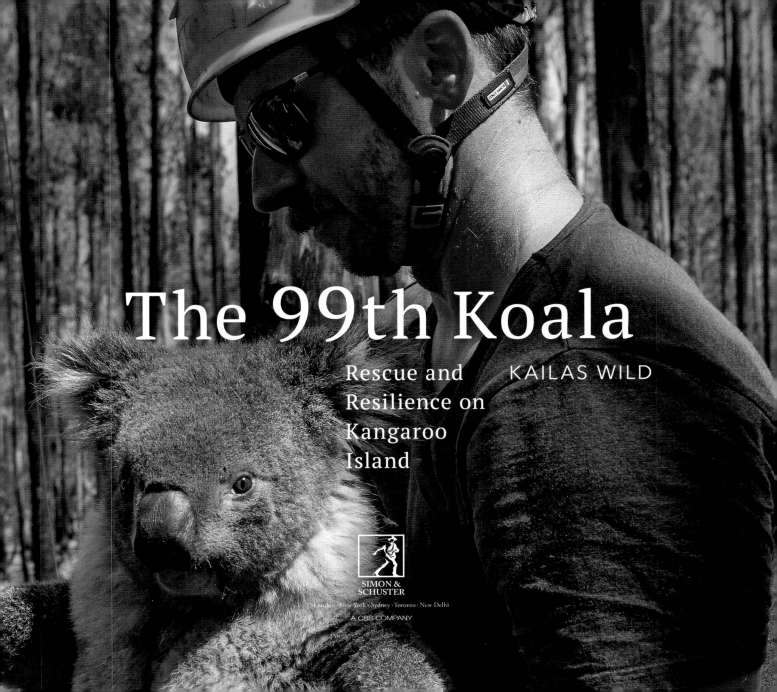

The 99th Koala

Rescue and
Resilience on
Kangaroo
Island

KAILAS WILD

SIMON &
SCHUSTER
London · New York · Sydney · Toronto · New Delhi
A CBS COMPANY

Australia's Black Summer bushfires were absolutely devastating. A combination of unprecedented heat and dryness meant that fires took hold with an intensity not seen before, and without sufficient rain, they felt unstoppable. Between June 2019 and February 2020 over 12 million hectares were destroyed. Every state and territory was affected – almost every person in the country was touched in some way.

Maybe you were one of those Australians living in the bush under threat of fire. Maybe your town or city was blanketed by the thick deadly smoke, which even drifted across the Pacific Ocean to New Zealand, turning skies there hazy yellow. If you were lucky enough to have escaped both, then chances are you were anxious about someone who hadn't been. As a country, our hearts went out to those whose safety was threatened, who lost their homes, and most of all those who lost loved ones. At least 34 people died.

We all shared the profound sense of grief at the loss of over a billion of our unique wild animals, along with their habitats. The number was, and still is, beyond comprehension.

For months we all felt helpless, myself included.

This is the story of what I did in response to that feeling – to try and help wildlife, and also myself. The seven weeks I spent on fire-ravaged Kangaroo Island helping rescue koalas were some of the most gruelling but rewarding of my life – an experience that has changed me in ways I'm still learning about.

Fire

My first encounter with the destructive nature of fire was at the age of ten:
I arrived home from school to find fire engines on our 12-acre bushland
property. A small fuel reduction burn had smouldered underground for days
before bursting into life and threatening the house when everyone was out
except my 80-year-old nan. I'll never forget my nan telling me not to worry
my mum, who was at work at the time, and later my mum being as shocked
that she hadn't been told as she was by the fire itself.

A couple of years later, a candle I'd left alight in my bedroom led to the room
burning to the ground. Luckily, it was separate from the main house – but I
can still remember the sound of glass exploding and how scared and helpless
I felt as I watched on, completely incapable of doing anything to stop it.
The experience drew a line under my childhood.

The Black Summer's megafires also moved me onto a different stage of my
adult life.

My direct contact with the fires began on 13 September 2019. An ecologist friend of mine, Mark, was helping fight the Bees Nest fire that threatened the rainforest adjoining the World Heritage Mount Hyland Nature Reserve, on the Mid North Coast of New South Wales. I went up to help. For a week, alongside the property owner Rosie and other community volunteers, we used dry, manual techniques to hold containment lines, clear around rough-barked trees to stop fire travelling up their trunks into their canopies, put out fires that were edging their way through rainforest and took shifts throughout the night to ensure the fire hadn't managed to jump. I'm an arborist by trade, so I helped reduce the major fuel loads in the fire path and clear burnt trunks that had fallen across access roads and evacuation routes. We managed to save some small patches of forest, and Rosie's house survived, but 50,000 acres were lost in that fire alone.

Cool temperate rainforest is typically cold and damp as the name suggests, and seeing it burn barely out of winter was a major, terrifying warning signal for what was to come as summer approached.

My second encounter with the fires was closer to home, north-west of the Blue Mountains at Running Stream. On 18 December, my then-partner Ella's family were preparing for the Palmers Oaky fire which was approaching their property. With winds expected to pick up in their direction, I drove up from Sydney to help them defend their home.

By the time I arrived, the NSW Rural Fire Service had managed to do a strategic backburn in the valley a few kilometres away, which limited the immediate threat. That gave us some more time to reduce the fuel loads and make sure the place was as prepared as possible if the situation worsened. Towards the end of the day the outlook improved and I decided to return to Sydney in case the fires burning further down the valley, near Lithgow, cut the road.

As I drove home, it felt surreal to see the fire getting closer and closer to the highway. Later that night the road was indeed cut.

Two days later, the conditions deteriorated significantly. Ella's family had been forced to evacuate and the fire burnt up to the front door. The house was saved only because the RFS arrived in the middle of the night.

Going back to work for myself as an arborist in Sydney, wearing a mask to protect against the smoke became a standard part of my Personal Protective Equipment. I felt lucky not to have asthma or to be in danger like so many people to the north, south and west of me. But I also felt worried about the affected communities and guilty for not doing more. I'd been a volunteer for the SES – State Emergency Service – for four years, so I put my name down to assist with their Bushfire Information Line, a phone service that provides updates on unfolding emergencies, and volunteered for out-of-area deployments as a chainsaw operator to support the RFS in the fire grounds. I also freed up as much time as I could to help locally in the suburb of Marrickville with requests for assistance – mainly storm damage – while other members of the unit were away supporting the RFS as radio or flood boat operators and capacity was lower than usual.

For me, the feeling of being powerless to help was the worst part of the bushfires and volunteering in whatever way I could seemed to be the only remedy.

On 3 January 2020, and then again on the 9th, two major fires devastated two thirds of Kangaroo Island, off the coast of South Australia, wiping out native forest, farmland, countless wildlife and killing two people.

The day the second fire tore across the island, I was volunteering as part of an SES strike team in southern NSW, assisting in communities that had been all but completely destroyed by fire – places like Lake Conjola where to survive, people had taken to boats or even driven their cars into the water. Where people had died, trapped in their houses. By the time I arrived, the immediate threat of fire had been replaced with health and safety hazards like exposed asbestos, unstable trees, smoke and mental health issues.

The most important thing our team could provide was the reassurance that help was at hand. People's lives had been turned upside down – with nowhere to live, in a state of shock, vulnerable to new hazards and health risks – but the thing that threatened to destroy their spirits was the feeling they'd been left alone to deal with the wreckage. This was the first time in months that I felt I could really do something; strange as it sounds, it was the first time I felt alright.

After returning home, my plan was pretty much more of the same – get back to work and give the SES as much time as I could. I'd seen the footage of the Australian Defence Force (ADF) helping with koalas on Kangaroo Island, and when wildlife organisations put the call out for volunteers, my interest was piqued, but the volunteer response was so overwhelming that I thought nothing more of it – surely they had the help they needed, and I was best off at home.

Koalas

The first time I ever worked with wild koalas was in 2010, as a 25-year-old living in Brisbane, Queensland.

I was studying native animal rehabilitation at technical college, and every Sunday for six months I made the three-hour round-trip to the small town of Beerwah for my practical placement at the Australia Zoo Wildlife Hospital. My job was to help clean out the koala enclosures, which needed to be kept highly sanitised while the koalas recovered from whichever illness or injury had caused them to be brought into care.

Although I'd grown up in the bush in northern New South Wales, I'd never even seen a wild koala before. I found the experience of assisting them in their recovery incredibly meaningful and fulfilling. In particular, I felt extremely fortunate to help with the feeding of a koala named Evana, blinded by chlamydia and now reliant entirely on her excellent sense of smell and the assistance of humans. But I also became aware that there was a vicious cycle at work: the koalas came into care to be rehabilitated only to be returned to the hostile environments created by humans that had caused them to need care in the first place. I found learning about the threats faced by koalas at the same time as having their trust in this way at the hospital to be a powerfully moving experience and a pivotal moment in my life.

In fact, it was koalas that led me to tree climbing, rather than the other way around. After my studies at TAFE in 2011 I spent several weeks searching for, catching and tracking wild koalas on properties in central Queensland as part of a University of Queensland research project about the effects of climate change on koalas. Up until then I had been terrified of heights and couldn't climb a tree to save my life, but I watched as my teammates clipped into harnesses and using ropes, skill and determination, levered themselves into positions to reach and capture koalas we otherwise couldn't.

That said, I didn't start climbing trees myself until three years later. I was immediately hooked, but it would take many, many years of pushing through feelings of anxiety and at times terror, to conquer my fear of heights. After a couple of shots at further study, and some practical conservation work, in 2016 I accepted that university wasn't really for me and made the decision to become qualified as a climbing arborist. That's also when I joined the SES and began helping wildlife carers regularly – where tree work experience was very useful. By now, though, I was living in inner Sydney, which meant more time with possums than koalas – in fact, although I'd been trying to save their habitats from logging and the impacts of climate change, by 2020 I'd seldom seen a koala since I'd lived in Brisbane and it was ten years since I'd handled one.

Going to Kangaroo Island

It's 8pm on Tuesday 29 January 2020.

I'm at the Marrickville SES unit, sitting in a debrief of the entire bushfire season, when out of the blue, I get a message from a wildlife carer in Sydney. She's asking if I know anyone on Kangaroo Island who can climb trees – someone there has found an injured koala that can't be rescued from the ground.

My first thought is: me. It's pretty impractical – I'm really far away, for one thing – but immediately I know I want to help. And since I don't actually know any climbers on KI, maybe it's not as crazy as it sounds. I reply that I don't know of anyone but maybe I can help?

After a few messages back and forth I step out of the debrief to take a call from a wildlife volunteer on Kangaroo Island. Ren is from an animal welfare organisation based in Japan and he wants me to fly down as soon as possible. I appreciate the urgency of the situation, but I know from previous experience that if I fly, the minute I get there I'll wish that I had my ute and all my gear. I decide that either way, I'll leave tomorrow and I figure I'll be gone for a week or two. I make a mental note to reschedule everyone who's booked me in for tree work in the immediate future and then drive home.

When I get there, I call Ella at her parents' farm, where we'd just spent a week clearing up burnt trees after the fires. I let her know that I'm going to KI for maybe a couple of weeks and we talk about the flying versus driving conundrum. I decide that if the koalas have survived almost three weeks, an extra day so that I have my gear and mobility is worth it. Then I pack all my essentials: swag, clothes, camping gear, all my climbing gear, chainsaws just in case, spade and toilet paper. I post on Facebook that I'm heading to KI which makes this crazy idea real. I set my alarm and manage to get a few hours' sleep.

At 4 the next morning, after a strong coffee, I set off.

This is the first time that I've driven straight across from Sydney to Adelaide. My map app says KI is 1540 kms away – 20 hours' drive, with a few breaks. It's a bit daunting, but I can roll out the swag whenever I need. Before long I'm out of Sydney and driving through the countryside – quiet roads with long, gentle views on either side. When I get to the Riverina, the pockets of remnant eucalypt woodland are a welcome respite from all the burnt trees I've been dealing with recently. In the rush I managed to forget my portable speaker so it's the radio or nothing for 20 hours.

As the hours tick over and the scenery becomes flat and repetitive, I start to wonder why someone on Kangaroo Island would need to reach out as far as Sydney for a tree climber. What's the state of the rescue effort? Maybe it's because of my experience with the SES, but I've assumed the response is being co-ordinated in some way. Aren't there teams of volunteers to find surviving animals and hospitals to treat them?

After about eight hours I get to Hay, a small town just under halfway to Adelaide. It's midday, I'm pretty tired and have started to wonder exactly what I'm getting myself into. Kangaroo Island is still a long way away – what if I arrive to find that my help isn't really needed and I have to make the 20 hour trip straight back home?

I pull over on Hay's main street, now seriously wondering whether I should turn around. Driving another 12 hours with a head full of these doubts would be horribly punishing if not unsafe. I delete my overzealous, affirming Facebook post that now has replies of encouragement and I wonder: how would I feel if I headed back home?

I can't seem to go in either direction, so I spend a good couple of hours calling everyone I can think of who might be able to confirm what the situation on the ground is really like, and whether another tree climber is needed at all. I call the wildlife organisations that I know of and think might know something, but they don't. I call South Australia Parks and Wildlife who give me the impression that everything's under control but recommend I try Kangaroo Island Wildlife Park. So I call them and speak to someone at the front desk who tells me the owner is flat out and too busy to talk to me right now. I leave my number and hope for a call back.

Feeling even more uncertain and wishing that I'd made these calls before I'd started the drive, I give Mum a ring for advice. She mentions that she saw an organisation called Humane Society International (HSI) helping koalas on KI in the immediate aftermath of the fires and they might be worth a try. The person I speak with at HSI tells me that someone's just come back from KI – they'll pass my number on. But now I've managed to miss a call from KI Wildlife Park and when I call them back, the phone rings out. Have I just missed my one chance of finding out if I'm really needed or not?

Frustrated, I head over to get a coffee from a cafe called the Black Sheep. The name resonates with me for some reason. Then my phone rings – an unknown number. I answer. It's Georgie from HSI. Thank goodness, finally someone else who might actually know what's going on.

I explain my situation to Georgie. She tells me about what she experienced on KI and I'm reassured – it sounds like there's some co-ordination to the rescue efforts, and that might be enough for me to slot in in some way. I'm extremely relieved. This one conversation has turned my doubt into determination to finish the very long drive. I even feel happy with myself for rushing off as I did because now I'm already halfway there.

It's about 2pm by the time I leave Hay and with my renewed enthusiasm
I continue to drive south-west across flat country. Suddenly at 6pm it
occurs to me that if I want to be on KI tomorrow morning, I had better
book the ferry from Cape Jervis. To my great relief there's space available
on the 7:30am ferry. So, certain that I can get on to the island, and certain
enough there's some way for me to be useful when I arrive, I drive straight
to the ferry terminal, arriving at about 10pm. Then I roll out my swag in the
tray of my ute, set my alarm and sleep the night under clear skies.

Driving off the ferry at Penneshaw on Kangaroo Island, in the still, cool morning, the only hint of the disaster is a single Army tent pitched on the side of the road. Here, there's nothing to indicate that two thirds of the island has been affected by fire.

As I drive out of the small township, however, the radio announces another day of 42-degree Celsius heat with a severe fire danger on the island. Although the fires have been contained there are still hotspots that the SA Country Fire Authority are concerned could flare up. I hope I'm not going to be one of those people who makes things a lot worse while thinking they're helping. A scene of me trying to rescue a koala and then needing to be rescued from fire myself plays in my head. Apprehensively, I drive on.

Just before the turn-off to the town of Parndana, I pass an Emergency Services command filled with vehicles on standby for what could unfold this weekend. It confirms what I heard on the radio and reinforces what I saw in my imagination.

Continuing towards the Kangaroo Island Wildlife Park, I soon start to see the impacts of the bushfires. All the vegetation either side of the road has been burnt and the fields beyond are empty and blackened. But it's not until I drive west of Parndana that the true extent of the devastation reveals itself.

The First Koala

I meet up with Ren at the entrance of the wildlife park. He's dressed casually but for a fluorescent yellow vest and although he seems tired, he's friendly and enthusiastic. Ren wants to check out an area where he found a koala the previous day and where he believes there might be more. When I see his hire vehicle filled with equipment, I feel relieved that I've driven down: there's no way I'd fit in his car, let alone any of my climbing gear. I immediately realise too, that neither Ren nor I have all the necessary equipment to catch koalas, such as animal carriers and flagging poles. Aside from needing to source additional equipment, my instinct is also to meet people who are involved with the co-ordination of the wildlife rescue effort before going any further to ensure I'm not doing anything that makes things worse.

Not really sure what to do or who to speak with, I walk up the driveway towards the wildlife park and what looks like a house. Gum trees line the left-hand side of the drive, and because I'm in the habit of giving pretty much all trees a once-over, I look up – and see a healthy koala, sitting almost at the top of one of them.

My first Kangaroo Island koala! It doesn't look like it needs any help at all, but still, it feels like a good sign.

I hang around near the front of the one-storey brick home. There are loads of towels, water bottles and animal carriers piled up that look like they've been donated to the park. Then vets and Australian Defence Force reservists begin arriving for work – and I realise that the images I'd seen of soldiers nursing koalas had come from here. The park isn't a small, informal part of the rescue response – it's a major one. I reckon I'm in the right place.

Before long, a bloke in a zookeeper's uniform appears. He seems pretty friendly and introduces himself as Daniel. When I explain why I'm here, he says I'm best off speaking with Sam. I hang around a bit longer, chatting with Daniel, who I learn is Sam's brother-in-law. He came over from Victoria to help Sam immediately after the fires, about three weeks ago.

Ten minutes later, Sam arrives. He's dressed similarly to Daniel – shorts, short-sleeved shirt and a cap. I repeat my story for Sam, straightaway sensing that he's wary of a new person. I do my best to assure him that I'm keen to do whatever is most helpful, even if that means turning around and going home.

My openness to help by not aggressively trying to help seems to put Sam a little more at ease. My feeling is that he's had to deal with a lot of people with varying degrees of experience and usefulness wanting to get involved. It seems that he's pretty close to being done with new people. It emerges that for the past three weeks Daniel, Sam and Sam's partner Dana have been working around the clock to cope with many hundreds of koalas and other animals that were casualties of the fires, as well as keeping their business running. Despite this level of exhaustion, somehow they still have it in them to give another stranger who's appeared on their doorstep out of nowhere the time of day.

I'm shocked at the casualty numbers Sam and Daniel are talking – tens of thousands of koalas gone, certainly hundreds if not thousands more injured and now possibly starving. The immediate rescue response following the fires has shifted down a gear – and there doesn't seem to be a formal process or dedicated rescue co-ordinator. No-one has enough capacity for that.

My offer of assistance is accepted and Sam lends me the equipment I need as well as kangaroo feed in case I come across hungry roos.

With these things, I can get started.

Handling Koalas

That morning I follow Ren west along the Playford Highway. On the way, we pass where local bush pilot Dick Lang and his son Clayton, a plastic surgeon, died when their car crashed after it was overcome by fire. We pass more burnt, empty fields as well as burnt timber plantations that go on and on, eerily uniform and devoid of life. We take a left onto a dirt road and after a short drive, arrive at the burnt plantation Ren's identified.

I get out of my car and the smell of dead animal takes me back to being in Lake Conjola nearly a month ago. I take a few steps and for the first time in my life, see what a burnt koala looks like. In one way, it's no more shocking than the rest of the devastated environment I'm already confronted by, but it's surreal – furry animals that live high in trees instead lying on the ground, without fur and turned as black as the trees. Although they're beyond our help, I can't help paying attention to each one we come across. They don't look like koalas anymore and I guess they aren't. For some reason there are more towards the edges of the plantation – perhaps because the ones towards the centre have been burnt to nothing.

We spend a considerable amount of time walking up and down rows and rows of completely blackened trees, scanning the canopy and the grounds. I notice there are small patches of burnt remnant vegetation and small dams towards the middle of the plantations. I check for any signs of life around a dam and am surprised when a Wedgetail Eagle flies off from it but after a decent search of the area, it's clear no living koalas remain.

Slowly coming to terms with this surreal situation, we next try an area of plantation closest to the wildlife park, where a small section of green trees survived right on the edge – what we come to call a 'green slither' – and where Ren knows a number of koalas remain. It makes sense that the surviving koalas would either be in the unburnt trees or have sought them out for food after the fire had passed through.

One of the first things we see is a very small, unburnt koala joey on a branch only about a metre off the ground. It looks healthy but the fact that it's so low in the tree, and that it isn't old enough to be fully independent, concerns me. I call Daniel on my mobile for his advice, and he recommends we bring her in.

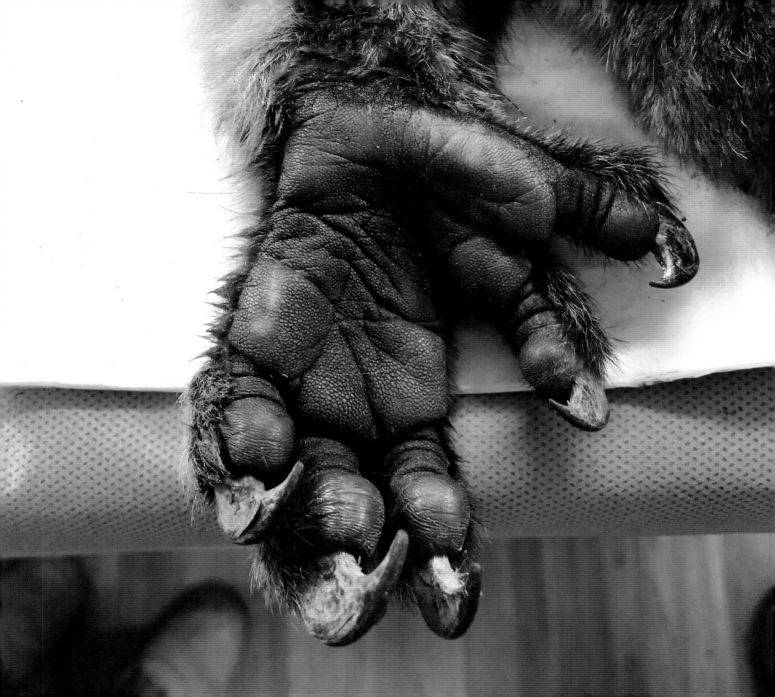

Ten years ago, I learnt to handle wild koalas by holding them by their forearms with a towel. This allows you to remove their grip from the tree and because their forearms are the strongest part of their body and can support their weight, there is less chance of injuring them. Wearing gloves and using a towel protects you from the sharp claws on their hind legs and from their teeth. I'm told the way they handle them here on KI is to hold them by the scruff of the neck with one hand and support them under their bum with the other. In theory, this means your hands are completely clear of their teeth and all claws. Still, I use my familiar technique: the small koala is easily managed, and we get her in the carrier quickly.

After the koala is safely stowed, we inspect two others we can see higher up in nearby trees. One looks big and doesn't have any obvious signs of burns or malnutrition. But the other has a burnt coat and looks very skinny.

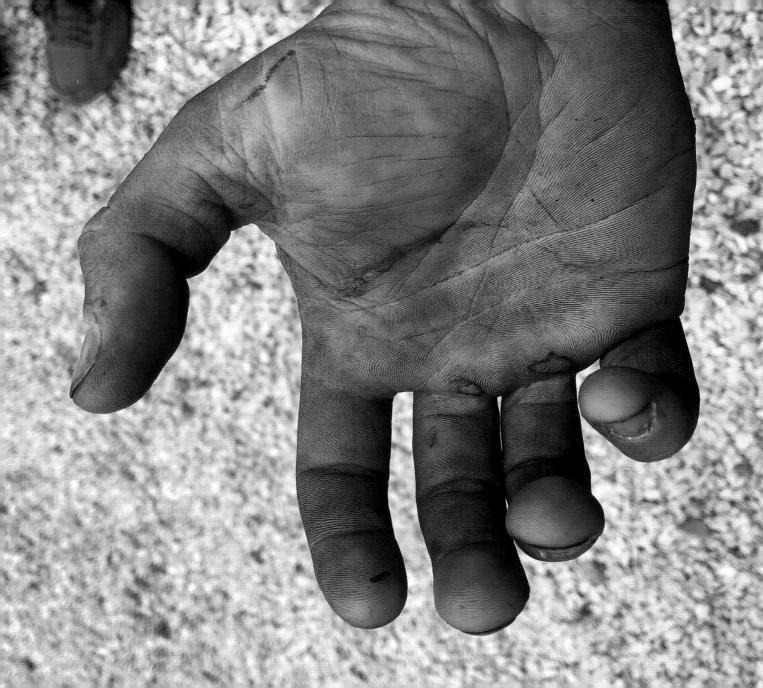

To my astonishment, as I'm looking at the koala with the burnt coat, the large koala climbs down from his tree and walks a few metres behind me before heading up the tree I was looking at. Both Ren and I notice that although he looked OK from a distance, his hands are burnt. So when he's about shoulder height up, I grab him by both forearms and remove his grip from the tree. He is stronger than I remember koalas being. Probably because southern koalas grow much larger than their northern relatives. He struggles in my grip and to hold him I have to place him on the ground. I quickly appreciate the benefits of handling them by the scruff and decide that from now on I'll do it that way. It'll take more than just Ren and myself to catch the skinny koala with the burnt coat with any efficiency, so we have to come back later with help.

Taking these two koalas in is my first visit to the hospital.

The hospital is set up in a small Army tent, staffed by vets from different zoos, wildlife organisations and the ADF. One half of the tent is occupied by two treatment tables and the other is divided between an admissions workstation and floor space filled with washing baskets containing koalas either awaiting or recovering from treatment. I watch koalas on treatment tables having burns attended to, mindful not to get in the way as I absorb what I'm seeing.

A soldier with the Reserves is helping to coordinate koala hospital logistics. Bree was deployed to KI on 4 January after the first of the two fires. She has more koala scratches on her arms than I've ever seen before but she handles the koalas with a confidence and impressive decisiveness that can only come from significant (and by the look of it painful) experience. Together we transfer the koalas out of pet carriers into the temporary enclosures where non urgent cases are able to calm down before being seen by the vet team.

There is a lot to get my head around and it's quite overwhelming but essentially there is the well-resourced hospital and the less-resourced rescue effort and I feel confident that I can find a way for my skills to be useful as a rescuer.

After seeing the koalas' accommodation, I leave feeling like they're in very good hands. My own accommodation is the most affordable motel room in Kingscote – a small 4x4 metre room about half an hour from the wildlife park but next to shops and essential services.

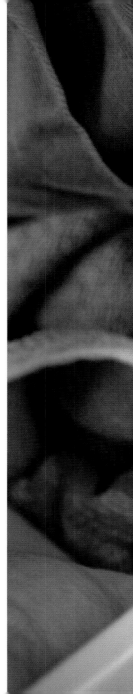

How Are We Going To Do This?

Back home, my work as an arborist can be pretty hazardous. I often have to deal with trees that might be compromised, where a falling branch – or complete tree failure – can be fatal. Add in climbing with chainsaws, wind and the surprises that trees often contain (bees, wasps or grumpy creatures with claws) and the result is that taking a little extra time to plan a job can prevent a great deal of pain.

On my second day on the island, KI experiences its most substantial rain in years. Torrential: thunder, lightning, even a chance of flooding. It's hard to believe that just yesterday, I arrived on KI with a severe fire danger warning. But this elimination of fire risk is a great blessing for everyone and an excellent opportunity for me to better assess the koala situation.

Yesterday's approach seemed a bit hit-and-miss. Early in the month, in the immediate aftermath of the fires, there'd been teams of rescuers and a more coordinated – if reactive – response, but that's trailed off in the following weeks as the immediate emergency has passed. I'm seeing koalas in clear need of assistance but I haven't seen or heard anything to indicate there is a resourced or coordinated search and rescue effort. My instinct is to want to put some structure in place – to work out which koalas need the most help the soonest, and to understand how big the task might actually be. So I take myself off to do some exploring.

Since so many of the surviving koalas are in the burnt timber plantations, I drop into the headquarters of the company that owned most of them. Considering I've just appeared out of nowhere, they're extremely helpful – they don't want to get in the way of the koalas being rescued. They give me a map showing which plantations are eucalyptus and which are pine – because koalas only eat eucalypts I can rule out a number of them immediately. But still, seeing the fifty plantations to the west of the island, all affected by fire and each one about ten hectares in area, makes me realise just what a huge job we have in front of us.

I use the rainy day to complete a circuit of the plantations near the main highways. With so many of the trees now a dull grey, it's easy to spot any remaining green trees at the far edges of the plantations from the road. I mark these on the map. I assume that surviving koalas have headed to these areas for food, and that's why some of them are overcrowded – the little fresh growth remaining is being over-browsed, accelerating the decline of the already stressed trees. It's possible that soon there will be no green slithers of trees left and despite having made it through the fires, a lot of koalas are beginning to starve.

My plan becomes: identify all the green slithers; count the number of koalas and determine their condition; and monitor the condition of the trees. This information will help to prioritise which koalas need help first. Getting round to all the green slithers every three days seems reasonable and achievable. It's a massive task, but with a methodical way to start tackling it, I feel optimistic.

The first koala I rescue by climbing up a tree on KI is the first koala I've *ever* rescued by climbing up a tree. I'm with Sam, Stuart (a keeper from Australia Zoo) and Sharon, who has come all the way from the USA especially to volunteer on KI, and even though I know I've got the skills and experience to do this, it's still somewhat daunting.

The koala is in a burnt wattle tree in the backyard of a private property that managed to be saved from the fires, and he hasn't moved in a number of days. Wattles aren't koala feed trees, and even if they were, this one doesn't have any living foliage on it anyway.

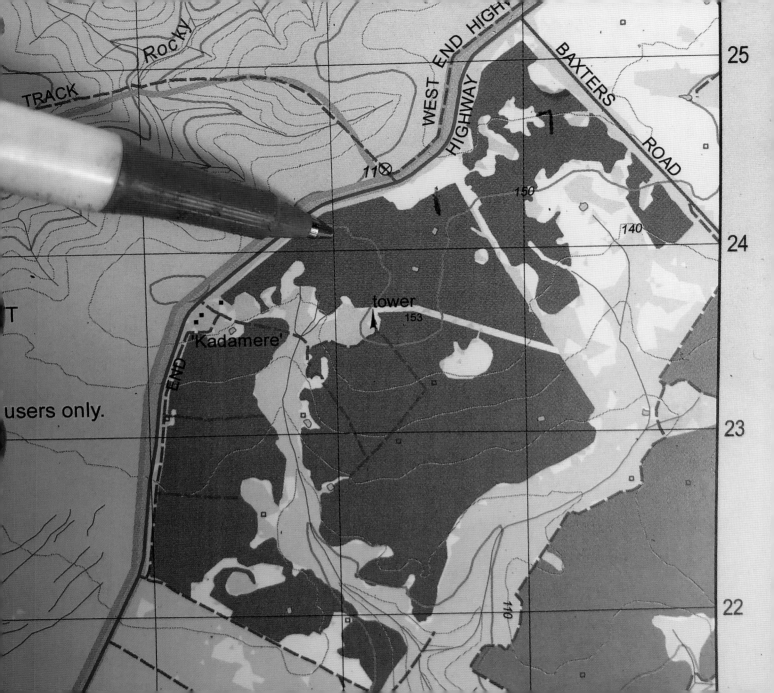

It's not a huge tree, and the koala's too high up to reach with flagging poles from the ground. There are a number of stems and a lot of smaller dense branches to climb through, which makes things tricky for me, but gives the koala a few options.

I'm feeling good about the chance to show Sam that I really can do what I've promised. But I'm also feeling the nerves. I've got to interact with a wild animal in a burnt tree six metres off the ground. And I've got a couple of sceptical lookers-on.

Constantly aware that the tree has been burnt and is potentially weaker than usual, I climb as high as I can. The koala's still about a metre and a half up above me, on a different stem, and not loving my presence.

Extending the flagging pole, I wave the flag above the koala, creating an annoyance he wants to get away from. He begins to climb down towards me.

I keep waving the flag, repositioning it through the dense branches above the animal and the koala keeps descending. Slowly but surely, I'm coaxing it out of the tree. As it passes my position, for a moment we make eye contact and I'm suddenly hit by the sense that I'm in exactly the right place. I came to KI for a purpose. This is it.

I work with Sam, Stuart and Sharon to flag the animal all the way down to the ground. Back at the hospital the vets check him – despite his less than ideal habitat and immobility, he's in decent condition, and so he's released into an area that hasn't been burnt.

I can't think of anywhere I'd rather be.

The Hospital

The hospital consists of an Army tent that serves as admissions and veterinary treatment area, rows of enclosures for the first stages of the koalas' recovery, and two larger tree-filled enclosures for pre-release animals. There are vet teams and husbandry teams, as well as people to coordinate hospital logistics and people to make sure there's enough fresh leaf cut for 150 koalas each and every day.

There are koalas everywhere. They are waiting for admission, being assessed on treatment tables and recovering from sedation in washing baskets. The outdoor enclosures are filled with dozens of koalas at all stages of recovery. Sam and Dana's house is filled with dozens of orphaned koala joeys.

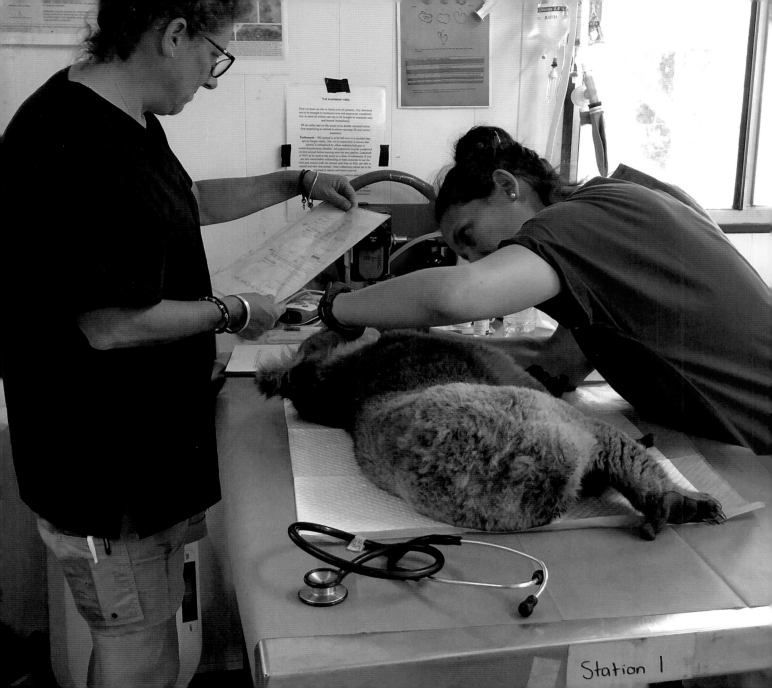

Station 1

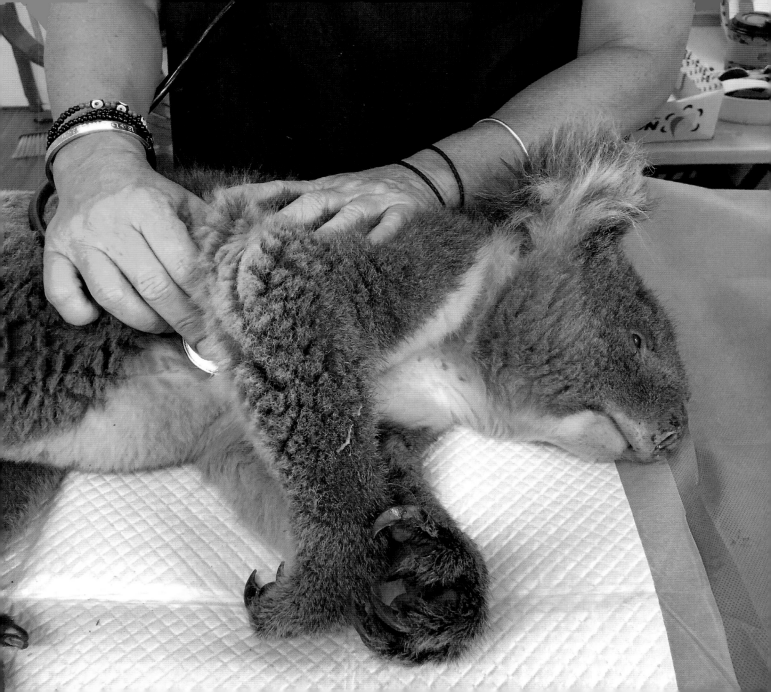

It's upsetting to see so many injured animals, but at the same time I get a great sense of reassurance every time I visit. The veterinary care is well-funded, well-staffed and functions at a very high level. Rotating teams of vets and nurses assess and monitor the health of the koalas that come into care, treat those who need it and then hand them on to specialist zookeepers and volunteers who help with tasks like cleaning, monitoring and feeding. Koalas are recovering thanks to the decades of experience of the committed and passionate people gathered here. It's a place of care and competence – a place of love, even – and I find it immensely sustaining.

Quite quickly, I'm getting to know exactly what help is needed and where I can best fit in. Within a few days, I find myself getting into a rhythm.

I help the zoo staff cut the day's ute-load of fresh leaf in the mornings –
fortunately, a plantation which had burnt last year didn't burn again this year,
so its regrowth is plentiful and easily accessed, almost as if it was designed
for this exact purpose. In fact, it's so essential that the idea of it not existing
is quite terrifying. Sometimes when we're cutting, we'll have a nice surprise
encounter with one of the lucky koalas that also know about this special spot.

I spend the afternoons monitoring tree decline and searching for koalas by
myself, following my system. Cam is one of the husbandry crew sent down
from Australia Zoo to cut leaf. We have an informal arrangement: I help
him in the morning and when I need ground support for a rescue in the
afternoon, Cam helps me.

The hospital is the public's point of call for koala rescues, so I continue to help Sam when a climber is required and when he's not flat out he gives me a hand with ground support. I really value the opportunity to work with Sam and as much as anything, it's a chance for the two of us to talk.

Sam tells me what it was like when they were under threat of fire and shows me photos and videos of the burnt koalas that came into their care in the early days. Knowing more about what he and Dana have been through, I'm filled with admiration for the way they take everything in their stride, like they have endless time and energy for people and wildlife. And yet I get the sense that, understandably, they need their lives back – starting with a loungeroom that doesn't have 30 koala joeys in it.

Coping

Out in the burnt plantations, when you're on your own, it's a very different experience to the comradery of being with other volunteers.

Each time I drive west on the Playford Highway towards the plantations, I have the same experience I had on my first day: I pass the skid marks swerving from one side of the road to the other that have been highlighted with yellow paint. The skid marks lead to a small shrine that stands as a memorial to Dick and Clayton Lang. I pass that spot two, sometimes four times a day, and think about how intense a fire would have to be to cause something like that to happen.

I also think about how the locals must have the same thoughts every day, and what that must mean for their mental health.

It's not until you drive down the West End Highway or along the South Coast Road that you see the absolute destruction wreaked upon Kangaroo Island's native vegetation. What remains is a sterilised, lifeless landscape for as far as the eye can see, followed by piles of large smashed-up trees that line the road for kilometres, broken only by driveways leading to what used to be people's homes. Total carnage. Driving through this devastated landscape every day, I'm focussed on finding koalas, but can't help feeling how overwhelming the toll has been on the rest of Kangaroo Island's precious wildlife. You can rebuild a house, but you can't rebuild a human life and you can't rebuild a complex ecosystem that's been completely sterilised by fire.

My SES deployment earlier in the month has helped prepare me for what I see and smell as I drive past destroyed homes and walk among burnt trees. But nothing can ever prepare you for seeing countless burnt koalas. The thing that *really* gets me, though, is seeing koalas that have died from starvation. That's what I'm meant to be here to prevent. Each one feels like a massive failure on my part.

I find it much easier to cope when I'm working in a group or with another person. Maybe it's because we're sharing the experience or because there are opportunities that distract me from the complete bleakness of where I am. Regardless, a certain level of desensitisation is required or this work would be impossible, which is no help to the koalas still alive. Quite often I feel like crying, which I tend to keep for when I'm alone. But there are times when I just can't keep it in, so sometimes I find myself weeping as I eat my breakfast, sitting in a café, or a mate calls me and I'll suddenly burst into tears. I've been driving with a journalist in the passenger seat beside me who's unaware of the pain in my throat and the tears in my eyes after we've come across a freshly dead koala. I'm aware that what I'm seeing is causing me trauma, so I try to write it down as a release, or simply allow myself to let out the emotion that needs to be let out. I can't think of anything worse than keeping it all bottled up and having it affect me worse later.

One unexpected outlet has been social media. I'd begun sharing what I've been doing quite openly since I got to KI, and people have been responding supportively. When I'm working alone it's helpful knowing that there are people out there who are following the fates of these animals along with me. It makes a world of difference.

Not Coping

When I'm out searching the plantations in the afternoons, most commonly I find koalas with burns to their ears, nose, hands and feet.

The easiest way to tell if a koala has been burnt is by checking from the ground – often by using binoculars – whether its ears are fluffy or not. I haven't seen it happen, but I imagine that when fire comes through the koalas respond by either coming down from their trees and fleeing or climbing as high as possible and bunching themselves up into balls. The longer hair at the ears is the first to be singed away. I hear a story of koalas jumping out of trees on fire. It really is a miracle that a lot of these koalas managed to survive the fires and a testament to their toughness that they've also survived the weeks following.

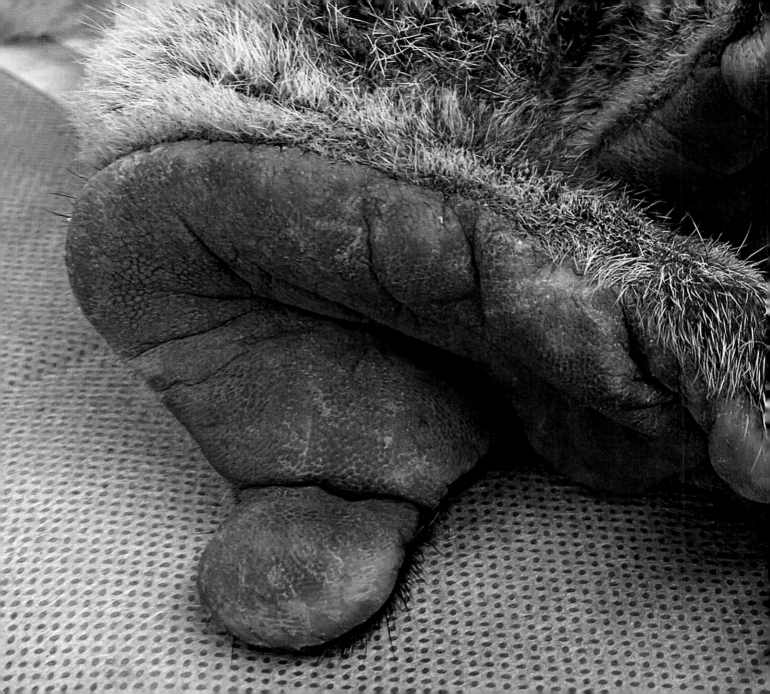

The worst injuries are burns to a koala's hands and feet. It's been almost a month since the fires now and in some cases those burns have become infected. That makes the animal very reluctant to move, especially if the infection has affected their claws, which they use to so firmly hold onto the tree. If I come across a koala that's been in the same tree for a few days, chances are that's what's happened. Something I'll never forget is grabbing a badly injured koala from a tree and its claws detaching because the infection was so advanced. It's bad enough putting a healthy or lightly injured koala through the stress of being handled, but to do it to one that's already suffering badly is extremely confronting and traumatic.

The first koala I rescue in this sort of condition is one I've been checking on for a week. It hasn't moved at all, even though the tree it's in is defoliated and there are much greener trees surrounding it. I already know, with a sick feeling, that the koala's in a bad way and that its condition is slowly but surely worsening.

There isn't a neighbouring tree tall enough to enable me to get higher than the koala, so I set up my climbing system from the base of her tree. As I'm doing that, she heads up to the very top. So she can move, but it must be very painful. The rescue is really rough: I manage to flag her down until she's below me but after this she refuses to go any further. That means I have to get her into a pet carrier eight metres in the air and lower her to the ground. It's so stressful I can barely see straight, but that's nothing compared to what I learn later on: that her claws are so badly damaged that she has to be euthanised.

The guilt of this really knocks me around. For days I'm left asking myself whether I could have done something differently, or if it would have been kinder to leave her alone. I continue to think a lot about whether I should be doing this at all. Eventually I learn from a vet that it was the fire that had damaged her claws irreversibly, not the way I handled her, and that leaving her to suffer infections and starvation would have been a much worse fate. Even so, the guilt lingers.

The Physical Toll

As well as being emotionally harrowing, the work is dangerous and tough, and that's taking a physical toll on me.

Here are some of the rules I follow for the safe climbing of hazard trees.

Inspect each tree thoroughly – it's always possible that fire has compromised the structural integrity of the trunk part way up, so test your anchor properly before you climb by putting all your weight on it and be mindful to continue inspecting the tree's condition as you ascend.

Assume that the trees surrounding a failed tree are likely to be compromised in the same way. One of the biggest dangers is that a tree's root-plate (its shallow network of roots that keep it firmly anchored to the ground) will have been affected by fire, which is something you can't always see. To minimise the risk of climbing a tree that's about to fall over, perform a pull test – loop a rope around a tree as high as you can and pull as hard as you can, watching for any movement in the root plate.

On the other hand, assume that the trees that are still green have been less affected by fire, with less chance of root-plate failure or structural compromise. This is handy because these are the trees that we find most koalas in.

Lastly, if possible, avoid climbing in strong winds. That just adds another force to an already weakened tree system, raising the chances of falling branches and trunks, and buffeting animal carriers, flagging poles and exhausted climbers. But it's not always possible.

As well as the unknowns that come with climbing burnt trees, stressing and handling wild animals in these trees also has its risks. In my mind, it's a given that every koala I handle will get its claws into my hands or arms, so the sooner I accept that the better.

The thing that you can't afford is to be bitten. Koala teeth are built to cut leaves and twigs, and because they spend most of their waking day grinding up leaves, their jaws are very strong. So a decent bite can easily see you needing stitches and put you seriously out of action. I prefer to have bare hands attempting a rescue because I find the protection of thick gloves is not worth the reduction in dexterity. So not only do you need to handle these animals in a way that minimises their stress, but also your own risk of injury.

That's not always easy in trees that are usually between 15 to 25 metres in height, with the koalas often pretty close to the top.

If a koala's only part way up a tree, the best approach is to climb a neighbouring tree to about the same height and use a flagging pole to try to get it to climb downwards. A koala's vision is poor but its senses of smell and hearing are excellent so using a material that makes a rustling sound for your flag is ideal. Then swing over into the koala's tree so it can't climb back up (although sometimes they try and we have a bit of a stand-off), and encourage the koala down until someone flagging from the ground can take over and catch the koala when it's within reach.

I've found this to be the least stressful experience for the animal, but it's pretty hard on the humans. It's most efficient to set a stationary rope as high in the tree as possible and ascend using mechanical devices that attach to your harness and grip to the rope, but to be extra mobile I use a second moving rope system that allows me to change my anchor point in the tree quickly and easily. But you're essentially hauling yourself up a tree with a rope looped over a higher branch and that's harder on the body.

I've been nursing a shoulder strain for six months – I'd almost recovered before coming to KI, but climbing trees this way, sometimes multiple times a day and carrying animal carriers and awkward gear, has begun to aggravate it.

And although I know I'm not without support, there's not another tree climber here.

If I find a koala high in a tree that I need help with, my first call is to Cam, after he's done cutting the animal's feed. And if Cam can't do it, I try Sam, but I know Sam's flat out at the hospital. They both do what they can, but even if they can come, I'm usually an hour's drive away so it's really not very efficient or sustainable. I'm starting to think that we need a team of two climbers whose sole purpose is searching for and rescuing koalas, and whose skills are interchangeable. But for now this will have to do.

Finding Joey Kai

The day begins with me sitting at a café, crying into my breakfast, readying myself for another long stretch of work.

After helping cut leaf in the morning, I continue searching through a burnt blue gum plantation on the southern coast, trying to assess how long the foliage on partially burnt trees will last. I come across a number of koalas with no obvious burns or signs of starvation – it's a great relief to see healthy animals, but I'm getting more anxious about what the future holds for them. I estimate that the trees have between two and three weeks of remotely edible foliage left. After that, the koalas will need to move or need to be relocated.

These trees have been slowly declining and don't show any signs of regrowth yet. In any case, the hospital staff have told me that the fresh shoots known as epicormic growth have a higher toxicity that makes them inedible for koalas. This makes sense from the tree's perspective, as a defence mechanism when it's trying to recover from fire, but from the koala's perspective, it's bad news.

After a couple of hours, I come across a tree with three koalas in it. The tree, although burnt, is still sound and two of the koalas look OK. But the third is very small, and her coat has been burnt. She's curled into a ball among dead foliage – the first injured, orphaned joey I've found and it hits me hard. I can't imagine she'll last much longer out here and it's pretty likely that she's sustained permanent organ damage and is too far gone to save. More than likely she'll have to be euthanised. I feel a real sense of urgency to get her back to the hospital.

It's not ideal to climb trees alone but I'm out of phone range, it's getting late in the day and help is at least an hour's drive away, so I try to work out whether I can catch her by myself. She's at the end of a lateral branch a third of the way up the tree – at least she can't climb any higher. I don't have any animal carriers either so I'll need to contain her in something else – I decide that because she's so small, she'll fit into one of my reinforced rope bags that can be attached to my harness.

I set up my climbing rope, prepare my flagging pole and put on my helmet and harness, now with a rope bag attached. My rescue plan is to climb to just above where her lateral branch meets the main trunk of the tree, and flag her back down the branch towards me. Then it's: grab her, in the bag, down the tree as quick as possible and off to hospital, an hour's drive away.

What sounds like a straightforward process can be incredibly fraught in practice. The entire time, the koala thinks it's being predated upon and the entire time I'm hyper-aware of the stress I am causing, trying to be quick while also safe, for me and the koala. I manage to get down without causing her to fall out of the tree and I sob driving back to the hospital with the small burnt koala that I'd ripped from a tree and shoved into a bag sitting next to me. I've never driven anywhere with such a sense of urgency in my life.

I carry my rope bag into the vet clinic, which is now in a small demountable building. Bree greets me and as I hand the bag over to the vet staff I burst into tears. Bree stays with me as we wait and watch the vet staff on duty, Paul and Di, gently check the joey's condition.

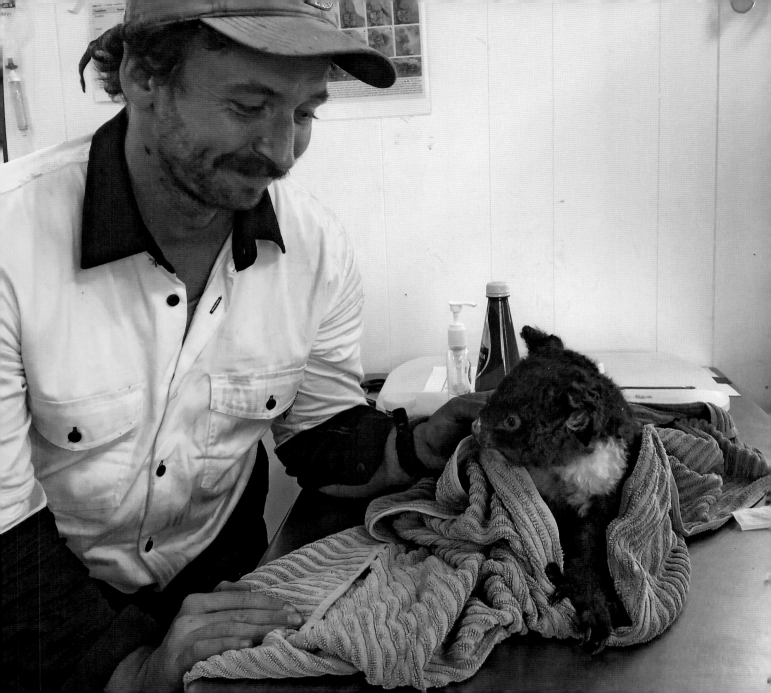

Eventually Paul explains that aside from the burns and some weight loss, her condition is not yet over the tipping point and her outlook is pretty good – they'll treat her and house her in a large pet carrier until she's recovered enough to be outside in a small enclosure. I continue to watch as they apply burn ointment to her ears and nose and a wave – an ocean – of relief begins to wash over me. It's just one koala, from among thousands, but to me she represents some kind of hope.

They finish her treatment and I'm allowed to give her a cuddle and she is named Kai.

After such intensity, I feel too churned up to go back out into the plantations by myself, so I take a day off to calm down and visit a beach at the north of the island that Sharon recommended I visit called Stokes Bay. On the way, I stop in at the hospital to check on Joey Kai. Someone has left a piece of paper on top of her carrier that says 'I'm new and will kill you' and I know she must be doing OK.

I almost manage to have a full day off when I get a call from Sam about a few koalas that he needs my help with.

Breaking Point

It's been nearly two weeks of ten to 12-hour days of this physically and emotionally draining labour without a day off and I'm starting to fray.

The koalas we help keep me going, but I spend my days alone amongst burnt trees and dead animals, and even the successful rescues are traumatic. The lack of resourcing and co-ordination is getting to me. The more koalas I find in poor condition and the browner the leaves on the trees are getting, the more urgent the situation becomes. And the more incredible it seems that there's no wider plan to do anything about it. I think about trying to relocate all the koalas which don't need immediate medical attention but will soon begin to starve: there are hundreds of them, there's no way I can manage that by myself. But no-one else seems to be thinking about it. I feel overwhelmed and very alone. I express my frustration and the need for more to be done in social media posts but as much as I'd like to be, I'm really not in a position to co-ordinate volunteers effectively.

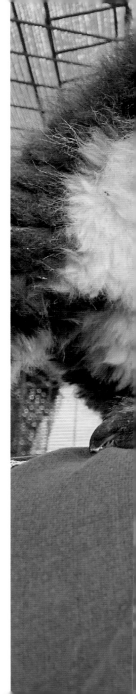

I really don't know how much longer I can keep this up and feeling desperate, I call Georgie from Humane Society International again and explain to her what I'm seeing on the ground. In fact I sob as I plead with her for help. She tells me that she'll speak with colleagues, and later that afternoon to my great relief, HSI announce their intention to return to KI to assist with search and rescue.

Later that evening, stressed and exhausted as usual, I get a message from
Alison, a carer from the KI Wildlife Network – someone I don't know, but
who's seen my social media posts – calling to check that I'm OK. And to tell
me that it's not just me out there looking for koalas. Several other people are
also committing a huge amount of personal time to trying to help wildlife.
It comes as a massive relief but also as a surprise that I didn't know this.
Good relationships are essential to the rescue effort and, like Sam, Alison's
been wary of individuals or organisations coming in out of the blue and
possibly jeopardising that. So we continue to talk, and over the course of the
conversation it becomes clear that we're on the same page and both want
what's best for the koalas and the community.

The call is intense and feels like a hug and a slap – I'm consoled and thrown
at the same time. Alison and I agree to meet up in person to work out how to
co-operate.

Getting Help

In the morning, after a short sleep, my head is clearer and I can see that I can't sustain what I'm doing alone, neither physically nor emotionally. The only solution is to find someone who can help to add to my capacity and fortunately I've managed to raise enough donations that I can afford to bring someone over and put them up.

The severity of the situation means it can't be just anyone. It's got to be someone I know well and trust completely. I try a few people I've worked with in the past – a big-tree climber, an environmental advocacy logistician, an SES volunteer – but all three have work commitments they can't break.

Then I take a long shot and call Freya. Freya was one of my trainers and mentors when I began learning how to climb, and she's been a friend and sometime colleague for seven years. She'd be perfect – she's got significant experience working in complex and stressful environments, organising people, coordinating logistics; she's calm, thoughtful and a bloody good tree climber. But she lives in New Zealand and I have no idea what her current commitments are.

Her response, though, is huge: she can come for two weeks. We arrange for her to fly over to Adelaide, pick up a hire vehicle and then catch the ferry over to the island – having my own ute has been a blessing and I tell Freya she needs the same independence.

It's hard to believe that I'll soon have a teammate. But now that my mindset's shifted, I reckon I just want to crack on immediately. So I message my local wildlife carers group in Sydney, asking whether anyone is able to help out short term. Deb – who I've met once before – is interested and has a few days free. We arrange for her to fly down.

One moment I'm alone and overwhelmed and the next, I'm still overwhelmed but Deb's here and Freya's booking her tickets, plus I'm starting to coordinate with the local wildlife network on KI. HSI are also on their way back and will help with the rescue effort for two weeks.

I realise that I'm actually a little anxious at the idea of someone I don't know very well coming in to such an intense situation with me in such a frazzled state, but to my relief Deb is amazing. She's a huge help with the logistics I haven't had capacity to deal with. While I'm out searching for koalas, Deb organises printing of large format maps that we can use to plan and monitor a co-ordinated search and rescue effort. Just as important is her generosity of spirit. Small things, like not minding if I'm running really late to meet her, are actually a big deal in my highly stressed state. I'll always be grateful for her kindness and helpfulness.

And there's other good news: I've finally met Jarod and Lisa, who are members of the KI Wildlife Network and – I've just learnt – have also been rescuing koalas and other injured wildlife on Kangaroo Island. The pair of them, often along with their two children Utah and Saskia, have rescued a total of 94 koalas since the fires began. They've lived on the island since 2012 and fortunately their property was spared from the fires. We team up to rescue two koalas that need a climber to reach and we work well together. So from now on whenever they find a koala that needs a climber, they'll call me.

This is the first time that I've felt any real sense of optimism since I came to understand the situation here.

Freya

When Freya arrives, during my third week on KI, my spirits are the highest they've been. I'm incredibly moved that a friend has travelled from overseas to help me. It's the first time I've seen a familiar face for weeks. It helps remind me who I am, outside of this unbelievable situation.

As I walk to meet her in the carpark of the wildlife park, I see that she's stayed absolutely true to form: no shoes.

Deb – who I've grown to trust and appreciate deeply – hands over the mapping side of things to Freya. We're splitting the plantations into two regions and allocating them to teams: Alison, Jarod and Lisa from the KI Wildlife Network; Erica, Georgie and Evan from HSI; and Freya and myself. The plan is for Freya and I additionally to assist the others with climbing when it's needed, as well as fetching down koalas who've climbed to the top of the hospital's soft release trees and need to be checked by the vets before their final release. We have structure, co-ordination, a supportive environment – I can feel my stress levels lowering.

There's just one small issue. Freya is a superstar logistician and climber but she's never interacted with a koala in her life. We don't have heaps of time so I have to get her trained fast – but because I've never taught anyone how to deal with wild koalas, we are both in the deep end. It's really not something that you can just explain without practicing so the hospital's soft release trees make a great training ground, where Freya can concentrate on interacting with the animals without worrying about the stability of fire-affected trees. I do a few demonstrations, and then Freya goes up several times and I talk her through her decisions.

Then we're ready to go.

Oliver

Freya and I work as well together as I'd hoped. Having a plan and a history of trust makes all the difference. We're able to get more than twice as much done and can cover places that I've never been able to check. In one of those plantations, in the north-west of the island, we find Oliver.

Oliver is two thirds of the way up a multi-stemmed blue gum on the corner of the plantation. The tree's got a tiny bit of green growth left on it, which the koala is eating, but has been heavily defoliated from browsing – he obviously hasn't left the tree in quite some time. His ears have been burnt and he looks very skinny.

We start to set up Freya's climbing system. She's still very new to interacting with koalas but this should be an easy one: climb up to above the lateral branch he's on, flag him down, I take over from the ground. But as we're setting up, the koala realises that something's happening. He heads back down his branch and straight up one of the multiple main stems. What first seemed like a good learning opportunity has now become a more complex rescue: the koala's got quite a few options, and can climb all the way to the top. Added to that, it's been raining, so the smooth bark is slippery and, just like the tree, a wet koala is a little trickier to handle than a dry one. I climb up with Freya.

Freya's using a fixed climbing system, anchored to a point just above where Oliver used to be. While it's easier to climb, it's much slower to change anchor points while in the tree. I can loop my ropes over higher branches and move around more easily, so I climb until I can reach Oliver with the flagging pole and encourage him down to where Freya can grab him. This will be the first time Freya's handled a koala in a tree. I watch as he backs down until he's right next to Freya. She grabs him by the scruff but he clings on and as they struggle, I watch as her hand gets within biting range. He continues to resist so I descend and help to release his claws from the tree and Freya is able to place him securely in a rope bag.

In the hospital, when the vets shave his fur to treat his burns, the extent of his injuries becomes more apparent. His ears are badly burnt and his hands have been damaged, although the wounds aren't infected.

I check on Oliver every day for the next week and share updates of his progress. Each time I come, he's happily eating fresh foliage in one of the enclosures and although there's no hiding the fact that he's been through the wars, he looks for all the world like he's on the mend. By this point, Freya and I have rescued about fifty injured or starving koalas – the circumstances of the rescue create an initial bond with an animal, but with Oliver, it's the way he's powered on that means I can't help but keep a special eye on him, checking in every day like I do with Joey Kai.

Then one day, when I'm bringing another orphaned joey into the hospital for admission, I notice a familiar-looking koala sedated on the treatment table next to me. It's Oliver. I'm deeply surprised and I ask what's wrong with him. The vets break the news to me. Although on the surface he seemed to be surviving, in reality he'd sustained permanent internal damage from smoke inhalation and malnutrition and his condition has slowly been declining.

They've decided that the kindest thing to do in Oliver's case is to euthanise him.

I stand by his side and hold his hand, sobbing as he goes peacefully.

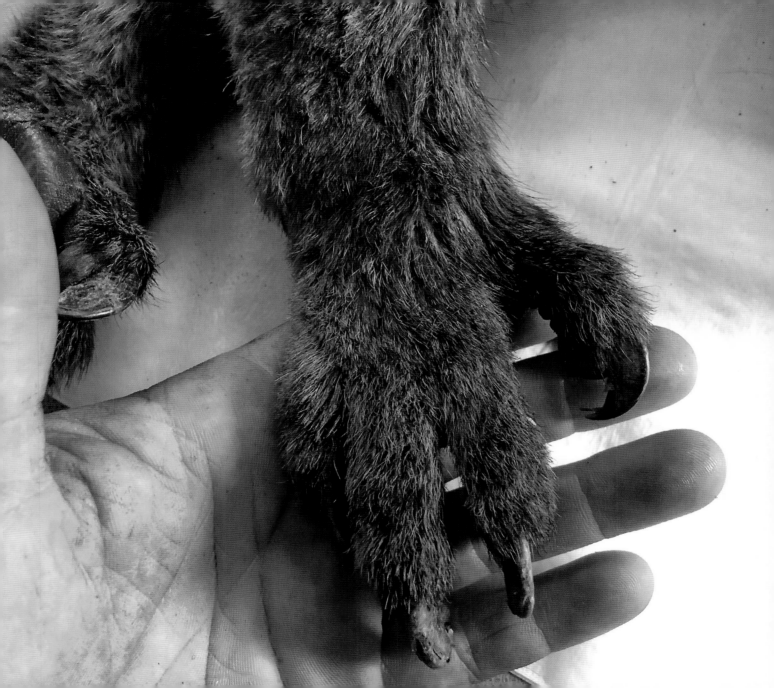

Burnout

I've now been on Kangaroo Island almost a month.

Freya has made a world of difference over the last two weeks and so has working with Jarod and Lisa and the HSI team. But HSI and the ADF have had to leave recently. As has Daniel, whose partner is about to give birth to their second child. Working in a team has felt completely different to working largely alone.
My social media updates have become less about me trying to get by and more about sharing the results of efforts that wouldn't be possible without the support and generosity of thousands of people. It means a lot to be able to share both the grief and the success that comes with this rescue work.

Thanks to people's donations, Freya and I have been able to hire a portable, elevated work platform, which can get us ten metres in the air pretty safely and quickly. It's a horribly nerve-wracking machine to use at first – even though we're used to being at height, both Freya and I feel pretty vulnerable being shot upwards on what feels to be an unstable platform (especially when the two of us are both in the basket), but once we've pushed past the fear, it becomes a valuable addition to the operation – only malfunctioning at height a couple of times.

Even with these positive developments, day by day the stress and fatigue are building for all of us. And then something happens that escalates it all and pushes me right to the edge.

Freya and I are helping to catch a mother and joey to relocate the pair to an area with adequate food. Dealing with two koalas at once adds to the complexity and raises the stakes if things go wrong. We've found that using a combination of climber and elevated platform is the most effective method for these rescues and although we've done it several times before, it's just as nerve-wracking each and every time.

This time, Freya's suspended at the same height as the koalas about 17 metres up a neighbouring tree and I'm below on the extended platform at about ten metres. Freya's attempt at flagging them downward has encouraged the mother with her joey to climb away and out to the end of her branch.

I don't have a pole long enough to help so I just watch as the mother sizes up a branch from a neighbouring tree and the next thing I know, she decides to jump.

She leaps – but she misses the branch she's aiming for. My heart stops. Mother and joey fall.

Down on the ground, 17 metres below, people scramble. The koalas survive the impact and are immediately on their feet, racing for the trees. The ground crew manages to capture the joey but the mum gets away and climbs 20 metres up a neighbouring tree. Although I have seen koalas take falls like this before and know they have evolved to survive them, it is no less gut-wrenching. We're all in shock.

While the joey is ferried straight to the hospital, Freya and I descend to the ground and I refocus to climb 20 metres to get the mother down. As I climb closer to her, I dread having to stress her again, but I'm also relieved to see that there're no visible signs of injury. I flag her down to my level, then past me and slowly work her down the main stem of the tree until she's within Freya's reach.

Mum and joey are reunited when we get to the hospital, and with no obvious injuries, they're left to calm down before being examined further. Finally we learn that both koalas are unharmed from the fall, and although they were in an area void of foliage, they were neither burnt or showing signs of starvation. They will be released in an area with sufficient food to sustain them both.

So the koalas are fine, but I'm done. My nerves are shot, and my shoulder's getting there – especially after that last climb for the koala mum when adrenaline look over. Freya and I decide that we need a break from KI, to switch off for a little. I want to fly home to Sydney for a few days, where I can see my physio about my shoulder and see a counsellor about my head. My partner Ella and I are used to being apart and pretty independent but she's been a rock for me this entire time and it'd mean a lot to spend some time with her however brief it may be.

Freya's found things tough, too. She's been confronted by the ethical and philosophical questions that should always arise when humans interfere with wildlife: should we be doing this at all? How do we know what's really best for the koalas? Her questions have forced me to think through my answers again, and although I feel I'm doing the right thing, Freya needs to come to that conclusion for herself. Some time away will let her do that. She'll visit her parents in Melbourne and decide if she's keen to return with me.

Being back in Sydney feels about as strange as I thought it would. My mind is still on Kangaroo Island, at the hospital with Freya, Sam and the team, and with the koalas starving in plantations. I feel quite overwhelmed by the normalcy of my home and the business of the city. I need to make the most of this time to run errands but I also really need to try to relax. Ella's busy with her regular life that I haven't been a part of for the last month but we get to spend a bit of time together and I can find out what's going on in her world. Although I'm an emotional wreck, I try to have the capacity to be supportive for the brief time that we have to spend together.

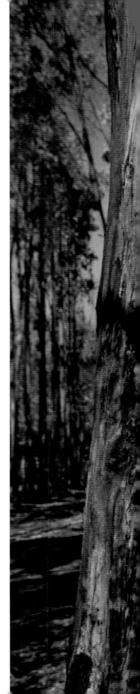

Fresh Start

I head back to KI on 4 March with a haircut, a music playlist and less pain in my shoulder. Although I'm feeling renewed, the refreshed perspective has also allowed me to feel a bit nervous about the intensity of what awaits me – the koalas still in the wild, running out of time, and Freya's decision to return or not will determine how well I will cope. My guess is that there's another month's rescue work left if we're able to continue working as we have been.

It's about midday when I open the door of my ute at Kingscote airport and I'm struck by how disorganised everything in the vehicle is – a picture of my state of mind. I cringe as I remember that it's about 5000 kms overdue for its regular service. Then the phone rings. It's a media company, asking where some footage I took is from. And then a journalist: am I back on the island? Can we come out with you? And where's the best place to stay?

Immediately, it feels like I never left. But thank goodness that I did – I feel that much better able to cope with the constant activity.

I go straight to the hospital to check in on Joey Kai. She's still by herself in her outside enclosure and doing well. On her admission form someone has written: 'Do not release without tree climber Kai'. I would be devastated to miss the opportunity to help release her and feel grateful to whoever wrote it. Her ears have healed and her nose almost has. Her singed coat has not grown out enough to provide waterproofing – apparently that will take another few months. She's nice and uninterested in me as a wild koala should be. I think I'll always feel a bit conflicted – I'd love to be someone that she grows to recognise, but I know that for her as a wild animal, the best thing is not to be humanised in any way. There's also a contradiction built into her treatment: I have to accept that the process of helping her might make her too reliant on humans to live independently in the wild.
And even if she is released, I'll be happy but also worried about the many other unnatural threats she'll face over the course of her life. There are no easy solutions.

Back in the small, crowded hotel room that Freya and I had been sharing, I feel that same loneliness that I did when I first arrived on KI. But then Freya calls. To my great relief she's decided that she wants to come back for another two weeks. We make a deal. She's resolved her questions about what we're doing, and I'm going to put us up somewhere more homely than a 4x4 metre room with no kitchen.

More good news: Sam and Dana have begun releasing rehabilitated koalas.

Turning a Corner

Sam has begun releasing rehabilitated koalas into privately owned bushland behind the hospital. It's an incredibly rewarding experience to see these animals climb up the tree trunks and be free again. The koalas who have only been in for a short time can't wait to get as far away as possible. But I notice that those who've been in care for longer and have had to get used to humans climb up a bit and then look back at us. You can't help but wonder what they're thinking. As time goes by, more and more koalas are recovering and being released.

We've had some rain and regrowth is starting in earnest. A number of the koalas we're finding in areas of completely burnt trees have been remarkably healthy. My new theory is that these are in fact the healthiest koalas in the plantations, on the move to new feeding grounds and stopping here only for a rest. No animal could have survived so long without food. So we decide that we'll focus solely on koalas in the green slithers, where they could have had enough food to survive this long, but might still be slowly starving and too malnourished or too injured to move.

In one of these green slithers, Freya and I find a koala at the top of a burnt tree, eating some of the regrowth. Up until now, we've been catching koalas in that situation because of our understanding that the regrowth is toxic. But this koala looks healthy – 20 metres up, hanging from one arm, munching away. I call Stuart, the keeper from Australia Zoo who left the week I arrived, to let him know what I'm seeing, and he speaks to a specialist koala vet – the changing situation is presenting us all with unfamiliar questions. The message that comes back is, if the koala's happily eating the regrowth then we can consider that food OK for that koala. Logical enough, but as far as I'm concerned, it's an incredibly significant development – it means we can make our rescue criteria much stricter. Our new rules are: we only search the green slithers, and to be rescued, a koala must be visibly burnt, emaciated and/or present signs of not having moved from their tree for several days.

For the first time, we don't have to assume that koalas in any part of the burnt plantations are necessarily starving and in need of help. This knowledge changes everything.

The 99th Koala

As well as these positive developments, there are still some extremely confronting experiences left for us.

Many of the koalas we're catching are increasingly healthy, and Freya and I are both not far off thinking we could leave them alone altogether. But after wrapping up for the day and heading out of the plantation we've been working with Jarod and Lisa, we come across a koala that's obviously been burnt and is now emaciated. It's late and we've been going all day but my gut feeling is to get her down. We know this is going to be bad: after all this time, any animal that looks in poor condition from afar is likely to be worse close up.

The tree she's in isn't terribly high but it's very thin. Freya climbs the neighbouring tree as high as she safely can and tries to flag the koala down from there. After some time, the koala responds, not by moving downward but by climbing higher, to where Freya can't reach her, and she lets out a haunting, shrill cry that I've heard a quite a few times now. It's a sign of severe distress. This is a miserable situation: the koala will slowly decline and die if we don't get it to hospital but getting her out of the tree will be pretty awful. Still, I can't see that I've got a choice – I decide to climb up her tree.

The tree hasn't been too badly burnt, so I trust that the trunk and root plate will hold. I set up my climbing system and ascend to where the tree trunk's no wider than my wrist in order to reach her with the flagging pole. She continues to cry, a hideous sound I never get used to hearing. Flagging her down feels violent and is the furthest thing from how I want to treat her but it works – she's backed down to my height to where I can now get her below me. This is when I notice blood on the tree. The burns to her hands have been severe enough that she's lost one of her claws and others are badly damaged. It's now been 45 minutes of stress that she's been put through. I don't want to put her through the pain of climbing all the way down to the ground so I check that I have a clear path to descend and grab her by the scruff of the neck, pick her off the tree and get down as fast as possible.

When I reach the ground and we contain her, I'm more overwhelmed than I've ever been after a koala rescue and I have to walk away to let myself fall apart – as the scene replays in my head. It's almost evening when we arrive at the hospital. We all know that her injuries are too severe for her to be rehabilitated. I stand by her side as she's put to sleep.

I'm feeling numb in a way I haven't been before. After what she'd survived and what I just put her through, I feel the need to respect and honour her life somehow. But I also want to respect the fact that euthanising animals is part of the job for wildlife vets and when aiding over 600 burnt koalas, a level of detachment is needed in order to cope. The best I can come up with is to place her gently into the pit dug out the back of the hospital and she softly rolls into place before we turn around and walk away – still emotionally frozen and processing everything that has just happened.

Although my intentions are to prevent greater and prolonged suffering, I will never feel comfortable knowing that my actions themselves caused suffering. Indeed, I think it's important to acknowledge this and accept it as something that comes with interfering with wildlife, letting it motivate me to focus on preventing the need for wildlife to be interfered with in the first place.

The Virus

In early March Freya and I watch and listen as COVID-19 slowly makes
its way to Australia and starts spreading. Communities that haven't begun
to recover from the bushfires now being threatened by COVID-19 is
particularly heartbreaking.

Although we feel far from the affected areas, the virus is evolving from
something of little concern to us to something that could turn our world
upside down. We need to do some rapid planning. We're both very far from
our loved ones and in the context of a pandemic, far from any real sense of
security. International borders are not yet closed but it's looking imminent,
meaning Freya needs to get back to New Zealand really soon. State borders
might close too. Sitting in the sun, next to a dam in the middle of a burnt
plantation, we eat lunch and formulate an exit strategy. We factor in the
foliage regrowth and improvement in koala health as well as our needs to be
safe in the face of what's coming.

Reviewing our map and spreadsheet, there are still a number of plantations
that have not been checked. We set a date of 18 March by which we have to
have checked all remaining plantations. We begin searching with a sense of
urgency not just for the koalas anymore, but for us.

The Last One

Things look to be winding up just at the right time. In the last week, we've found only two koalas we've had to rescue.

After checking plantations all day we find one at the very top of a 25 to 30-metre tree. Through binoculars we can see its ears and coat are singed and it looks emaciated. A large quantity of scats (droppings) at the bottom of the tree indicate that it's likely to have been in the same tree for a number of days, so it fits our criteria for rescue. Freya prefers to climb and with my shoulder still sore, that suits me.

As she ascends, the wind picks up significantly. All I can do is watch as the tree begins to sway, knowing exactly how she must be feeling. Freya gets to a point where she's got a good footing but isn't quite high enough to reach the koala. She asks me whether I think she can climb any higher. I reckon she can safely go another metre. The wind continues to gust at around 40 to 50 kilometres per hour. Freya manages to get the flag above the koala, who begins to move down, but then heads out along to the end of a branch. Suddenly, it's hanging below the branch, gripping to leaves only, swinging by one arm 20 metres up and swaying in strong wind. This koala is at seriously risk of falling.

As Freya and the koala sway along with the tree, I do the only thing I can think of and set up a tarp suspended a metre or so above the ground to catch it should it fall. Freya and I know all too well what can happen if we push a koala too hard too fast. The neighbouring tree is close and thin so Freya tries to pull it over to give the koala an escape route but to no effect. Using Freya's climbing rope, I send up a thick branch that she then offers as something solid for the animal to climb on to, again to no avail. By now it's been an hour. My tarp set up has grown to twice the area and we're out of ideas. We decide to encourage it to move up. Freya reaches towards it from below with a flagging pole and to our great relief, the koala responds by climbing up and onto the solid branch.

Nerves shot, I pay close attention while Freya begins working the koala down the tree. Finally, she is within my reach and I discover she is one very angry koala. I manage to place her into a container and Freya and I take a moment to gather ourselves before packing up and taking her back to the hospital where she spends the night in an enclosure calming down.

The next day the vets inform us that she is of acceptable health and that she also has a pouch young. As poor as her condition appeared at the time, she wasn't in need of assistance and the very real risk to the koala, her joey and to us have turned out to be unnecessary. This is the moment that we realise we're done: enough time has passed that any survivors from the fires are likely to be able to continue fending for themselves, and the risk of injury to the koalas and ourselves now outweighs the potential benefits.

We release the stressed mum as soon as possible back in the area where we found her. She is especially impatient and sprints all the way up to the top of a tree. It's the fastest that I've seen a koala move and it's a great weight off my shoulders to see her free again.

Leaving

From this point on Freya and I are in wrap-up mode.

To my surprise there's still a number of plantations on the list that haven't been marked as checked. More for our peace of mind than anything else, our goal is to get round them all by the end of the week, knowing that it's incredibly unlikely that we'll find any koalas that need our help. We drop by the hospital most mornings and help to recapture escaped koalas before heading out to the plantations. We meet our target and as we thought – and to our great relief – we find no more koalas that require rescue.

It's now 19 March and Freya and I, booked on the next day's ferry, drive to the wildlife park one last time to say goodbye to the people and koalas who have come to feel like family. To my relief, vet and now friend Flick offers to send me regular updates of Joey Kai's progress. Sadly, Sam is away for a couple of days so I don't get to say goodbye to him properly, but I have plans to return in the not too distant future when Joey Kai is ready for release.

After leaving the park, I spot a koala in a burnt tree to our left and I can't help myself – I pull over to check that it's ok. It's only a few metres off the ground in a small tree and I can easily and safely climb up to check on it without ropes. Its location is terrible but its condition is very good. The koala and I look at each other and for the first time since I arrived on KI, just for this moment, I feel incredibly calm and relieved in knowing that I don't have to interfere.

With a sense of relief and sadness, Freya and I leave Kangaroo Island for the mainland on 20 March. When we say goodbye at Adelaide airport, we promise to stay in touch and to continue to support each other in recovering from the experience we have just shared.

I start the long drive home to Sydney a different person to the one who drove to KI. I've seen with absolute clarity how all my seemingly separate skills and disparate life experiences enabled me to help the way I have. It's taught me that whatever I choose to put my energy into now – no matter how big or small – can count for something positive in the future.

It would have been a mistake to let the fear of failure or the pursuit of perfection prevent me from volunteering on KI but I've also been reminded that helping takes more than just good intentions. We need to act with integrity, thoughtfulness and empathy for others.

It seems clear to me if we're going to prevent disasters like the Black Summer bushfires from reoccurring and if we want any chance of preserving our world's incredible biodiversity, then we need to take bold steps to address climate change and to reduce our destructive impact on our natural world.

And we need to do it together.

Acknowledgements

I would like to express my deepest gratitude to each and every person – too many to name – who provided me with the emotional or financial support that enabled me to help on Kangaroo Island. A special thanks to my incredibly supportive editor Ben Ball who made this book possible.

Additional images

© Daniel Berehulak 2020, pp.5, 26–7, 44–5, 50–1, 57, 78–9, 85, 87, 96, 111, 115, 122, 125, 126–7, 129, 143, 164–5, 206–7.
© David Maurice Smith 2020, pp.2, 3, 20–1, 29, 42–3, 53, 58–9, 69, 70–1, 72–3, 75, 88–89, 95, 97, 115, 117, 146–7, 173, 182–3, 192–3.
© Michael Dahlstrom 2020, p.141.

Design: John Canty
Cover photography: Daniel Berehulak
Endpaper photography: Kailas Wild
(front endpaper); David Maurice Smith
(back of front endpaper; rear endpaper);
Daniel Berehulak (back of rear endpaper)
Printed in China by Asia Pacific Offset Ltd

First published in Australia in 2020 by
Simon & Schuster (Australia) Pty Limited
Suite 19A, Level 1, Building C,
450 Miller Street, Cammeray, NSW 2062

10 9 8 7 6 5 4 3 2 1

A CBS Company
Sydney New York London Toronto New Delhi
Visit our website at www.simonandschuster.com.au

Text and images © Kailas Wild 2020

ISBN: 9781760858094

A catalogue record for this book is available from the National Library of Australia

NATIONAL LIBRARY OF AUSTRALIA

HUMANE SOCIETY INTERNATIONAL
AUSTRALIA

A portion of the proceeds from the sale of this book go towards supporting wildlife conservation efforts in Australia

MIX
Paper from responsible sources
FSC® C136333
FSC
www.fsc.org